Trampoline Activities
for
Atypical Children

Bryant J. Cratty, Ed.D.
Professor of Physical Education
University of California, Los Angeles

Peek Publications ■ **4067 Transport St.** ■ **Palo Alto, California 94303**

GV
545
.C73x
1969

Copyright 1969
Peek Publications

Second Printing 1972

Manufactured in the United States of America

Contents

Chapter 1
    Introduction 1

Chapter 2
    Selecting a Trampoline 3

Chapter 3
    Pre- and Post-Trampolining Activities . . 7

Chapter 4
    Teaching Trampoline Activities 11

Chapter 5
    Safety Rules and
    Basic Orientation Procedures 15

Chapter 6
    Balance Activities 21

Chapter 7
    Agility Activities 27

Chapter 8
    The Body Image 33

Chapter 9
    Basic Drops 39

Chapter 10
    Complex Combinations 45

Chapter 11
    Thinking and Trampolining 47

Appendix
    Check List of Skills, Agility
    Exercises and Balance Activities 51

Bibliography 53

1
Introduction

In the middle ages court jesters entertained the nobles by jumping from springy take-off surfaces. During the 18th and 19th centuries circuses in the United States and in Europe contained tumbling acts in which acrobats utilized various kinds of springboards and canvas beds to add height, daring, and interest to their exhibitions. With the development of the collapsible trampoline during World War II, widespread acceptance was achieved and "rebound tumbling" was added to school physical education programs and to gymnastic competitions. During the middle of the 1950's "do-it-yourself" trampoline centers flourished for a brief period, but soon disappeared when it was found that the unsupervised practice of trampolining could be dangerous and without proper instruction in sound progressions of stunts, children taught themselves as much as they could and then lost interest.

More recently the trampoline has been looked upon with favor by educators attempting to improve the capacities of various types of atypical children. Some clinicians have attached magical powers to trampoline jumping, while others are less expansive in their claims for the effects of jumping on resilient surfaces.

I first became interested in the trampoline in college during my participation on the gymnastic team. Later, while coaching high school gymnastics and while training teachers at the University in gymnastic methods, I became more interested in the manner in which the human body could perform while relatively free from the earth's gravity for an instant. Eight years ago, while instituting a physical development program for neurologically-impaired retarded children and unfit normal children, one of the first pieces of equipment obtained was a trampoline. During the intervening years I, along with others, have become convinced of the value of this interesting device for the development of the perceptual-motor capacities of atypical children.

Many individuals working with the perceptual-motor capacities of children do not have a background in the basics of trampolining, and upon consulting books on the sport usually encounter material describing how one learns gymnastic stunts of moderate to high levels of difficulty. Independent of the acquisition of gymnastic stunts; however, it appears that the trampoline has a great potential as a developmental tool. Our clinical work with children has revealed that activity on the trampoline is potentially useful in the development of the body image, in the strengthening of anti-gravity muscles of the legs, trunk and neck, and in the improvement of locomotor abilities and balance. Moreover, various learning games may be played on the surface of this interesting device; games which may encourage serial memory ability, and creative thinking. Trampoline jumping is fun. Children derive a great deal of exhilarating movement for relatively little effort. They will tend to persist in the activity for prolonged periods of time, thus overloading their muscular systems and producing real change.

At the same time, imprudent use of the trampoline can lead to an aggravation of various muscular problems in children. Hyperactive children with difficulties in impulse control may become too highly aroused when bouncing and will require some kind of "calming down" activities after their participation. The manner in which the trampoline's bed rebounds can cause a slight to severe whiplash-type of injury to the back or neck region. With this in mind one section of the text contains pre-conditioning activities which should be engaged in prior to prolonged exposure to vigorous rebound tumbling. Thus with improper use the trampoline can overstimulate, injure or otherwise may not be helpful to children already beset with intellectual, motor and/or emotional problems. Throughout the text I have attempted to set forth warnings, to design educationally sound sequences of movements and to describe conditioning activities to be carried out before and after jumping on the trampoline, thereby providing both negative and positive guideposts to trampoline jumping.

The trampoline has been found to be a helpful "developmental tool" when working with children who evidence movement problems. Its use should be tempered with caution and should be accompanied by preconditioning activities as well as by activities following its use to "calm down" participants.

The large trunk and leg muscles are strengthened as the child jumps on the trampoline. In addition to balance, agility activities as well as games which require thought may be carried out on its resilient surface.

2
Selecting a Trampoline

The size of the trampoline should correspond to the size of the child. A trampoline too large for a light 4- or 5-year-old is not effective—he cannot depress the bed; while a heavier 65-pound 6- or 7-year-old requires a larger trampoline bed (5' or 6' by 8' to 10') in order to provide a challenge. Although the portable tubular-framed trampoline is most familiar, it is easier and safer to work with children on a pit trampoline. A pit trampoline consists of a regular bed placed in a frame over a pit in the ground which is deep enough to permit freedom of action.

Both kinds of trampolines, however, should have frames which are well padded, and should be located to provide sufficient overhead clearance to avoid injuries. At least 10 feet are needed (measured from the bed of the trampoline to the ceiling), with 15 feet being preferable. It is often possible to purchase used trampolines. If the reader is handy with tools much of the cost, such as the cost of the expensive frame, can be avoided by constructing the pit trampoline illustrated.

4 Trampoline Activities

If the capabilities of the children to be worked with indicate the possibility of learning advanced stunts, an overhead "spotter" is desirable. This consists of a frame placed on or over the trampoline which contains a pully system containing a spotting belt, to effectively support the child as he turns over forward or backwards.

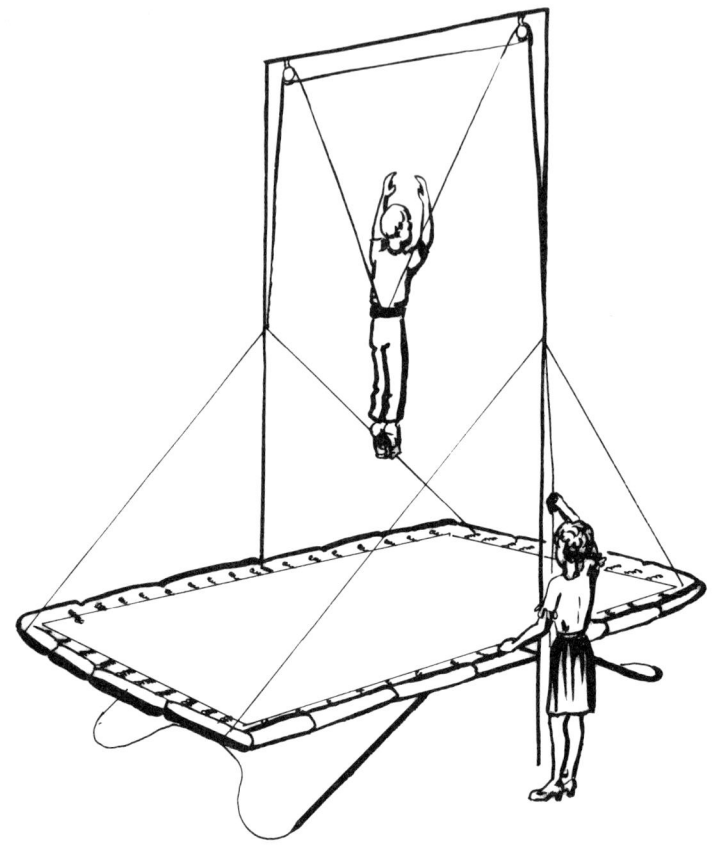

In most cases, however, this type of elaborate spotting equipment is not required.

Special care should be taken when storing the trampoline. If the pit trampoline is outdoors, a heavy water-repellent canvas should be placed over the bed and springs. If the trampoline is to be stored for a prolonged period of time, preservatives should be placed over the metal portions to prevent deterioration. The springs should be periodically inspected and replaced if any appear defective or worn.

It is helpful to have various markings on the trampoline. Many of the activities to be described in the following sections assume that two cross lines are placed on the trampoline bed...like this:

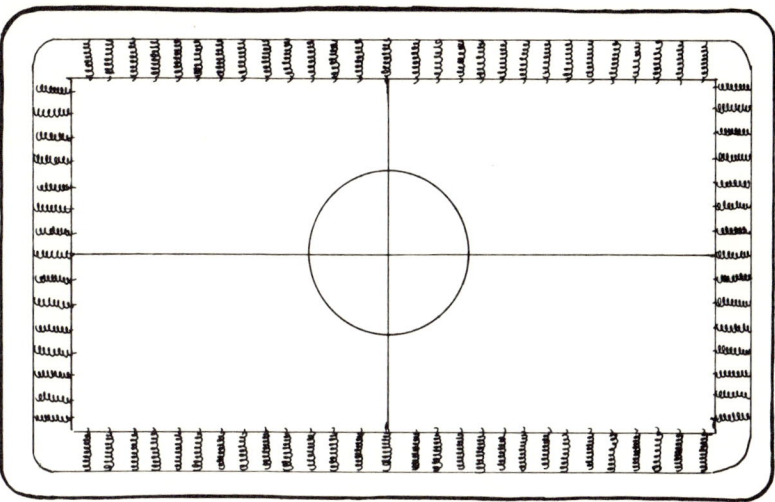

At least the center of the trampoline should be delineated by a target, and it is desirable to have both a target and cross lines, as shown. It is also desirable to have mats adjacent to the trampoline so that various conditioning and relaxation activities may be practiced before and after bouncing.

SUMMARY

1. The size of the trampoline should be compatible with the weight of the child. A child weighing up to about 50 pounds may use a smaller bed; a child weighing over 60 pounds should be provided with a full-size trampoline, if possible.
2. There should be sufficient overhead clearance, at least 10 to 15 feet for children doing elementary tricks.
3. The bed of the trampoline should contain a central target and cross lines dividing it into fourths.
4. Care should be taken to maintain the bed and springs in good condition, particularly if it is to be stored for a period of time.

3
Pre- and Post-Trampolining Activities

Prior to trampolining, two general types of activities may be profitably practiced. Exercises for the trunk, arm and leg muscles may be needed before the child's body can withstand the shock of trampolining. At the same time, activities designed to teach specific trampoline skills may be engaged in prior to mounting and jumping on the unstable bed. Following a trampoline practice period some atypical children may need various types of activities designed to lower their level of excitation to a degree appropriate for effective performance in classroom tasks.

Pre-Conditioning Exercises

To prevent possible injuries to the lower back, a number of back extensions should be performed prior to each trampolining session. This type of exercise promotes the trunk rigidity needed if the child is to jump very high when he reaches the bed.

The reverse sit-up, as pictured, should be done for six to eight repetitions, with each repetition held for two to four seconds. If capable, the child should be required to do from two to three sets (six to eight repetitions each) prior to each lesson. Added difficulty can be achieved by requiring that each repetition be held for increased amounts of time, by added sets, and/or by reducing the recuperation time permitted between sets. When performing these sit-ups, the ankles should be held.

Other conditioning exercises might include bent-knee sit-ups as shown. Again the repetitions should be held for two to four seconds, with sets of six to eight repetitions administered if the child is capable. These may be made easier if the child reaches forward with both hands, or more difficult by clasping the hands behind the neck as shown.

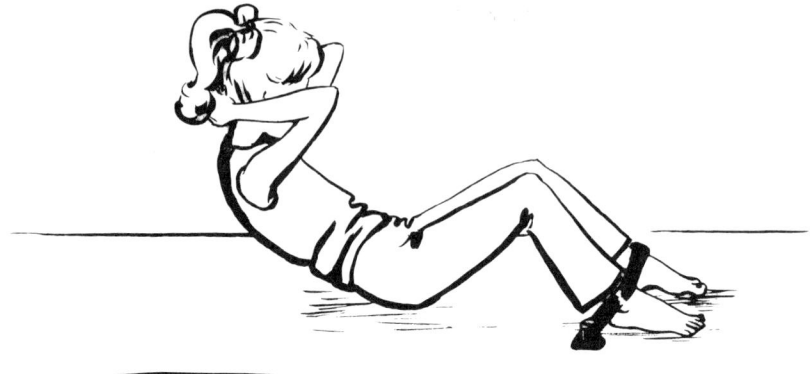

Slow stretching, particularly of the muscles in the back of the legs, is an important conditioning activity. The child may reach for his feet in a standing or a sitting position as shown, and attempt to maintain the stretch for several seconds, rather than bouncing as he reaches for his feet.

Selecting a Trampoline 9

A number of activities intended to make more efficient use of teaching time may be engaged in while a group of children are on the ground, prior to individual jumping.

They may be taught to jump upward with an arm swing upward and inward at the same time, similar to the action desired when ascending from the trampoline's bed.

The children may be taught to jump, and then "break" their landing by quickly bending their knees and lowering their center of mass, as is required when attempting to "kill" their bounce on the trampoline.

The various landing positions may be taught in groups on the mats prior to individual practice on the trampoline, thus shortening learning time.

Seat Drop

Hand-Knee Drop

Back Drop

Front Drop

All these positions should be practiced in groups on the mat as well as individually on the trampoline bed prior to jumping to them.

10 Trampoline Activities

Post-Trampolining Activities

Following a vigorous trampoline session it may be desirable to engage in a number of "calming" activities. Relaxation training consisting of alternately tightening and loosening groups of muscles and muscles of the entire body may aid hyperactive children to relax, after the stimulating fun provided by the trampoline.

This type of relaxation training may be engaged in as the child remains on the bed of the trampoline, or he may be placed on a mat, in a face up position. He should then tighten his arms, fists, facial muscles, trunk muscles and leg muscles and after each of these efforts attempt to relax them completely. "All out" tightening may be interpolated by attempts to "tighten one-half as hard as that," or "...one-fourth as hard as you can," and so on.

Following this relaxation training the children may be asked to see how slowly they can move in a number of tasks in order to further aid them to keep themselves under their own control. "Walk as slowly as you can from here to there!" "Let's see who can stand up the slowest!", "Who can draw the slowest line across the back?" and other activities initiated by similar directions may aid an over-aroused child to gain control of himself following his efforts on the trampoline.

4
Teaching Trampoline Activities

To teach a child to perform and to move on a trampoline, one should follow sound principles governing any type of skill training. A number of ways should be utilized to communicate the desired movement to the child, including a visual demonstration of manipulation of his body parts, and verbal explanations when necessary. Care should be taken not to over-instruct. Requiring a child to organize too much information too rapidly from an outside source, many times makes it difficult for him to perceive the sensory patterns emanating from his own muscular system.

Initial orientation to the trampoline will often require the instructor to join the child on the trampoline, and specific ways in which this should be done are described in the sections which follow. At other times the instructor should, while standing on the floor adjacent to the apparatus, attempt to "spring" the bed by pushing it downward with his hands in order to create movement which in turn will aid the child to perform more effectively.

Practice periods on a trampoline should be brief. About a minute is maximum for younger children so that fatigue, of which they are sometimes unaware, does not suddenly disrupt their movements and cause an accident. Children who are left to stand for excessive periods of time at the edge of a trampoline, particularly if they are distractable, will not usually prove very cooperative after a few minutes.

For most of the basic moves, initial practice should be given in the assumption of the landing position first on the ground, or mat adjacent to the trampoline, and then in the center of the bed without any bounce. The next appropriate step may be to mount the trampoline behind the child and to "spring" him gently to his feet by moving the bed with his feet. Following this kind of practice the child should be encouraged to attempt the various "drops" by himself, if undue fear has not been evidenced during the initial phases.

During the orientation periods, as the child is being taught to move his arms properly when jumping, it is often also desirable to mount the trampoline with him, and to guide his arms up his sides in front of him, as he attempts to leave the bed.

Several teaching techniques are helpful when working with atypical children with specific problems. For example, the blind child can be taught many basic stunts, but should be held in the spotting belt arrangement pictured below, in which each of two instructors holds a rope attached to a belt around the child's waist.

Stunts presented to the retarded child must be broken down into their basic components, whereas usually the same tricks, when taught to children with normal intelligence, need only be demonstrated totally and they are then imitated by the alert student. Prolonged demonstrations and verbal explanations, in excess of those needed or wanted by any child, are oppressive and will impede well-motivated learning. Generally, a child should be introduced to as much of the total skill via a visual demonstration as he is capable of organizing at one time.

Various sections of this booklet deal with the manner in which various concepts and percepts may be acquired through movement experiences on the trampoline. In all cases, however, it must be remembered that when a movement is designed to teach a concept, i.e., the world has a left and right relative to the child, that specific transfer from the movement to the concept must be taught. The child should be told why he is engaging in the various types of learning activities explained on the pages which follow. In this way he is able to build "cognitive bridges" between various components of his movement education program, rather than merely being trained like some kind of high-level animal.

One of the more effective ways to motivate children to do anything well is to be sensitive to their constant search for novelty and complexity. The same principle applies when the trampoline is used as an educational instrument. The instructor should be cognizant of the manner in which a given task may be made more complex to challenge his students' capacities. New tasks should be introduced from time to time as interest wanes in the familiar ones. Social approval for success from the other students and teacher, together with the introduction of tasks which are interesting and of optimum complexity (not too difficult or easy) are the best ways to keep motivation and interest high.

In the final sections of the booklet it is attempted to outline just how higher level thought processes may be stimulated by various kinds of movement games on the trampoline. When engaging in this type of practice, the sensitive instructor should attempt to insert himself as little as possible into the learning process. He should ask the child to demonstrate how many ways he can devise to do the task. Later, when children demonstrate the ability to create interesting modifications of the task, the instructor might pair off children and have one evaluate the efforts of the other. At the highest level, if the students are capable of making these lower level decisions about modifications in the learning process, the instructor may ask the students to invent trampoline games within specific limits imposed by the teacher. For example, "Here is a rope and a piece of chalk. Invent a game using the trampoline."

SUMMARY

1. Trampoline practice should consist of short, frequent "trips."
2. Motivation will remain high if the novelty and complexity of the tasks introduced challenge the capacities of the participants.
3. Specific modifications should be introduced for various types of atypical children. The disturbed child may need more manual directions and emotional support while the instructor is also on the trampolines. The blind child will usually require special spotting belts and ropes, as pictured. The retarded child will require special help in-involving careful analysis and breakdown of the more complicated movements requested of him.
4. Best teaching is not over-teaching. Too many directions

may interfere with the child's attempts to organize his own movements. Too much structure and direction may discourage thought about the activity on the part of the participants.
5. The instructor should demonstrate, tell and manually manipulate the limbs of the child when it is appropriate. At the same time the child should be encouraged to engage in trial and error practice at appropriate times.

5
Safety Rules and Basic Orientation Procedures

A trampoline is a reasonably safe piece of equipment if proper teaching progressions are utilized, if the child is properly guided during the learning process, if he is not permitted to become fatigued while bouncing and if several basic orientation procedures are followed closely. While the elasticized bed may appear deceptively safe to some because of its apparent "softness," it does something the "hard" floor or mat does not do--it jumps back after being depressed. Thus landing properly is critical, or this springing back can severely strain joints, pull muscles, or even break bones.

Initial safety procedures should be followed prior to the child's mounting the trampoline. He should be conditioned, so that his body will take the shock of the trampoline's bed. The trampoline frame should be properly padded, so that slight inaccuracies will not be "punished" as the child lands on aluminum or steel bars.

After these previous activities have been carried out and basic jumping and "killing" of the bounce procedures have been practiced on the matted floor, the child should be taught to mount the trampoline. If the trampoline is one of the common folding types this can prove formidable to the smaller child. He can often be taught to climb up chains from the side, or be provided with an incline ladder to crawl up.

After proceeding to the bed and across the springs the first

thing a child should do is to crawl around the bed on all fours, under the direction of the instructor. If the child is severely retarded the instructor should remain with him at this point. The child should be instructed to find the edges by crawling to them, and then to find the center of the trampoline by looking for the intersection of the lines which have been provided.

After a period of time has been spent in this crawling kind of orientation (the length of time depending upon the nature of the child) he should be encouraged to stand in the middle of the trampoline, and gently move the bed by lifting his arms upward and toward the front, circling inward and upward, and outward as they descend, keeping them in front of his body as shown here.

As the bed moves, he should be asked to "stop" his bounce by quickly bending both knees and lowering his hips; i.e., by assuming a sitting position, without actually encountering a chair. The effectiveness of this practice can be noted by observing how quickly the bed stops moving. This step also may be guided manually by the instructor, facing the child and manipulating his arms by holding his wrists.

A Child Shown "Killing" His Bounce

Some atypical children (a child with moderate cerebral palsy or a blind child), may be encouraged to make the initial up and down movements of their bodies while remaining on all fours, and then to stop their movements by quickly falling on their stomachs, moving their arms and legs quickly to the front and to the rear.

After several successful attempts to stop his bounce quickly (in one "sit") without actually leaving the bed, the child should next be encouraged to swing his arms upward more vigorously and permit his feet to leave the bed. After two or three bounces in this manner, he should be similarly asked to "kill" the bounce by executing a quick knee bend as he reaches the bed with his feet.

During these initial efforts at bouncing, the arms should be swung in small arcs in front of the body. If the arms descend so that when viewed from the side the hands are behind the vertical plane of the body, the child will tend to wobble backward and forward out of balance. These initial bounces should not be made

too high, about a foot or less is high enough even for the larger children. The child's body should not be high enough to induce a lack of integration between body parts, i.e. it should not "loosen up" in the air...for if it does it is possible that a mild or moderate neck or spinal injury could occur as he reaches the taut bed upon landing.

Trampoline jumping is not really the same type of jumping action as is carried out on the ground. Rather it is a "riding" upward of the tension and rebound created in the bed by the performer's body weight. This "riding" is done with the knees, back, stomach and neck regions tight as the body contacts and leaves the bed. Additional lift is obtained by vigorous arm action, and the hard upward thrust of the arms as the child leaves the bed gives more impetus to the hard extension of the legs as they leave the bed.

The legs should be shoulder-width apart as the feet contact the bed on each bounce and should be brought together in the air, and the legs tightened. The arms should move together inward and upward as the body rises, and should descend in a small circle downward and outward as the body descends to the bed; the hands should be about level with the waist as the body contacts the bed and then lowered further as the body depresses the bed, arriving below the waist at the lowest point.

The child's eyes should be looking at a single point mid-way on the frame at the end of the trampoline for greatest safety. Permitting the child's eyes to "wander" as he jumps can lead to inaccuracy and incoordination in the air, although many children find it difficult to maintain a constant "fix" on a target while jumping.

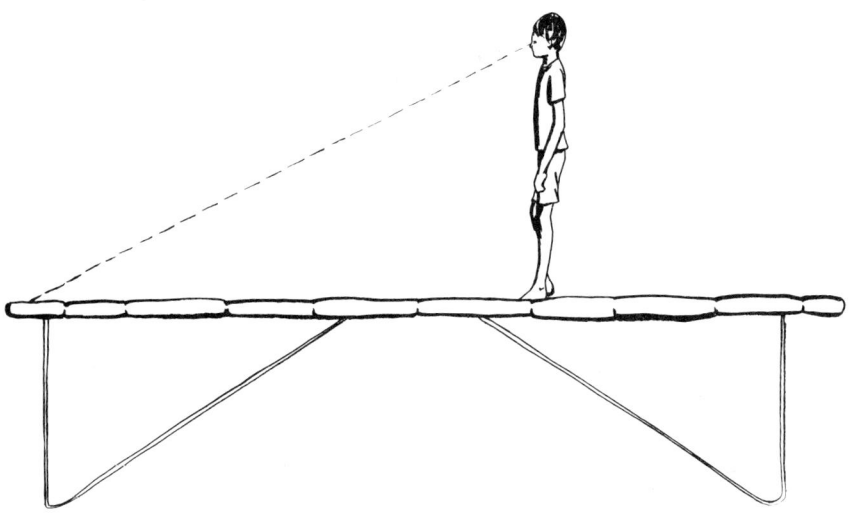

The child should jump in the middle of the trampoline facing the shortest end. During this initial orientation period, after the starting and "killing" action has been learned, the child should be asked to jump slightly off center a foot or two and to stop his bounce, to the left, right, front and back. Later he should be asked to jump and make first one-quarter and then one-half turns to the left and right, with an immediate stop after the turn is completed ..."jump and turn...jump and turn...," etc., is an activity which will be discussed later in the section of the monograph dealing with the training of the body image.

Leaving the trampoline is fraught with peril. The child is often fatigued, and the quick change in resiliency from the jumping surface of the elastic bed to the hard floor will often result in severe ankle injuries. A child SHOULD NOT JUMP FROM THE TRAMPOLINE TO THE FLOOR. Rather he should carefully lower himself to a sitting position on the edge of the bed, swing his legs across the springs, and then, holding on to the frame, slowly lower himself to the floor with the aid of the instructor, if necessary.

The paramount safety procedure, however, when working with atypical children on the trampoline is a thorough assessment by a physician, prior to confronting a child with the apparently harmless bouncing game. Children with moderate to severe movement problems can often aggravate their conditions by bouncing and being "jolted" on the unstable surface offered by the trampoline. Hernias can be induced, ankle tendons can be injured, back problems can be aggravated and other muscular and orthopedic conditions can be worsened if an instructor is too expansive in the type of child he selects for participation. A physician, not a trampoline instructor, should select children for this unusual activity. And if children who are selected are noted to experience any discomfort, they should be permitted to rest, and be re-evaluated by a qualified physician, prior to getting on the bed of the trampoline again.

In general only one child should be allowed to jump on a trampoline at a time. If two children jump at the same time a real danger exists that the lighter one will be drawn toward the heavier child with injurious contact resulting. At times an experienced trampoline instructor may wish to have two small children bounce in separate portions of a large trampoline. A variety of motivating games can be played with this arrangement, i.e. jumping back and forth in squares while facing each other, etc. However, this should be done only on an extremely large trampoline and should be carefully supervised.

SUMMARY

1. A physician should select and evaluate children prior to participation on the trampoline.
2. Initial orientation as to jumping, stopping and dropping positions should be carried out on the mat.
3. Crawling around the bed should be an initial introduction to the trampoline for most younger atypical children. They should be permitted to discover the edges and the center in this position and should be accompanied by the instructor if necessary.
4. Initial bouncing should not involve leaving the bed of the trampoline, and may be in an all-fours position, or in a standing position depending upon the movement, intellectual and emotional capacities of the child.
5. Proper ascent and descent to the trampoline should be taught.
6. Proper bouncing techniques, methods of "killing" the bounce, and methods of moving off-center and regaining the center of the bed should be taught.
7. Proper bouncing should include circular arm action (both arms moving together) in circles in front of the body, with the eyes fixed on a point at the end of the trampoline to which the child is facing. The arms should circle upward and inward on the ascent, and outward and downward during the descent.
8. The instructor should be sensitive to signs of discomfort and fatigue as the child bounces.
9. Bodily control should be taught prior to attempting any more complicated activities.
10. Only one child should be permitted to bounce on a trampoline at a time.
11. When a child is bouncing on a trampoline, other children, if they are capable, should be arranged around the trampoline facing the performer, ready to push him back on the bed if he bounces too near the edge. The instructor should also serve as this kind of spotter.

6
Balance Activities

It has been proposed that the trampoline can be used as a developmental tool. By using the trampoline in this way it is possible to practice a number of balancing activities using the bed of the trampoline in various ways. The unstable base provided by the elasticized bed is a more difficult surface upon which to engage in various static balances than is the floor, (i.e. standing, balancing on one foot, etc.). Various line-walking tasks using the lines on the trampoline should aid in the acquisition of better moving balance.

Balance is an important attribute underlying the performance of a number of locomotor activities, hand-eye coordinations and sports skills. Its improvement will usually be reflected in increased proficiency in a variety of perceptual-motor tasks. Balance involves coordination between both sensory and motor systems; the eyes, vestibular apparatus in the inner ear and the muscular system cooperate in both obvious and subtle ways as a child attempts to orient himself to gravity. It has been found that balance ability can be improved in children with mild to moderate movement problems using the types of tasks outlined in the pages which follow.

Assessing Balance Abilities

To determine whether a child has a balance problem several simple tests may be given. For example, he may be asked to stand on one foot on the floor to evaluate what is termed static balance.
1. A seven-year-old should be able to posture on one foot without moving for ten to fifteen seconds.
2. A five-year-old should be able to balance on one foot for from four to six seconds.

If the child five years of age and over cannot balance on one foot, but instead must quickly lower the other foot to the ground or engages in an excess amount of arm and foot movement, i.e.

"dances" in place, it may be assumed that improvement in balance is needed.

To evaluate moving or "dynamic" balance the child may be asked to walk a two-inch-wide line from 10 to 15 feet long on the floor. By four years this kind of task should not prove difficult for a child if he has no balance problem. By the age of five a child should be able to walk a three-inch-wide balance beam placed about six inches high and about 10 feet long, placing one foot in front of the other. A four-year-old should be able to do this also but may slide one foot forward, keeping the other foot behind his first foot as he moves across the beam.

Static Balance

Using the center of the bed, the child can be asked to balance on one or both feet with various kinds of visual and/or motor "stress" imposed. Generally the order of difficulty in these kinds of tasks has been found to be as follows.

Standing Balances

1. Standing with eyes open, one foot in front of the other, feet shoulder-width apart.
2. Standing with feet on a line, shoulder-width apart, eyes open, arms free to balance with.
3. Feet together, heels together, eyes open, arms free to balance with.

Balance Activities

4. One foot balance, preferred foot, eyes open, arms involved.
5. One foot in front of the other, on a line, heel to toe balancing, eyes open, arms balancing.
6. Feet and heels together, arms folded, eyes open.
7. Heel to toe standing position, arms folded, eyes open.
8. One foot balance, preferred, arms folded, eyes open.
9. One foot balance, non-preferred foot, arms folded, eyes open.
10. Heel to toe balance, eyes closed, arms aiding the balance.
11. Eyes closed, heel to toe, arms folded.
12. One foot balance, preferred foot, eyes closed, arms utilized in the balance.
13. One foot balance, preferred foot, eyes closed, arms folded.
14. One foot balance, non-preferred foot, eyes closed, arms folded.

This order may be different for different children. For example, we have found sometimes that children with visual perceptual problems may balance better with their eyes closed than with them open. When they cut off their distracting and unstable visual field they function better, depending only upon kinesthetic feedback mechanisms.

Hand and Knee Static Balances

The general order of difficulty is as follows:

1. Three parts of the body touching the mat, i.e. two hands, one knee; both knees and one hand, etc.
2. Two parts of the body on opposite sides of the body touching, i.e. left hand and right knee.
3. Two parts on the same side touching, i.e. right knee and right hand.

24 Trampoline Activities

When introducing a child to these activities the instructor should attempt first to ascertain just which ones offer a challenge to him. These three or four activities within each sequence should then be introduced and be held from four to eight seconds, with a rest of about the same period of time permitted between each effort. This should be repeated several times; and then if a child is capable, he should be asked to invent his own static posturing positions, i.e. "Balance on the trampoline with three parts of your body touching it," etc. During these "creative explorations" on the part of the child, the instructor should remain cognizant of the reasonable order of difficulty so that the child may be given more specific directions if it becomes obvious after several minutes hesitation, that the child either cannot think of anything, or that he over-compensates by attempting tasks too difficult.

In addition to these static balance activities the child may supplement balance-beam work with "trips" down the lines on the trampoline. He may be asked to do several things as he traverses the longer of the two lines marked on the bed of the trampoline... for example:

1. Walk the line watching your feet.
2. Walk the line watching the point at the end of the trampoline. Also watch the point when jumping.
3. Walk the line and step carefully over the rope placed across the line at several points.

4. Walk through the hoop held over the line.
5. Walk the line while watching a moving point at the end of the trampoline (i.e. the instructor's moving hand). Easiest, of course, is to watch a point moving in a vertical plane. It is more difficult to watch a point moving from left to right while walking forward.

Balance tasks of the type described above can aid children having moderate balance problems. The tasks should be selected according to the child's capabilities. Both moving and static balance tasks should be utilized, and those on the trampoline should be supplemented with similar ones practiced on the mats and balance beams. Balance may be improved by placing visual and motor stresses of various kinds upon children as they attempt to orient themselves to gravity while statically positioning themselves in some way or when moving along a narrow base. More stressful, of course, are tasks involving static and dynamic positionings on the unstable base found on the bed of a trampoline.

Care should be taken not to "overstress" children in the tasks described in this section. For example a child with orthopedic problems should not be subjected to these activities unless approval is received from a physician. A child with a defective knee joint should not be asked to posture on one leg on a trampoline (nor probably on two legs) as it is likely to aggravate his condition.

SUMMARY

The trampoline may be used for several types of balance activities. Static balance either close to the bed in various hand-knee positions or when standing may be practiced. Additionally, various moving balance exercises may be executed using a line on the surface of the trampoline. Balancing may be made more difficult by requiring a narrower base of support, i.e. standing with the feet closer together, narrowing the walking surface by using a narrower line, or in various ways placing stress upon the visual-motor integrations needed to balance well. The latter can be done by requiring the eyes to move as the child attempts to remain in a static position.

Balance ability is an important attribute underlying a number of movement skills. If a child evidences a balance problem when asked to posture on one foot or to walk a line, remedial efforts should be made and if intelligently applied should induce positive change.

7
Agility Activities

Agility involves the abilities requiring the coordination of the larger muscles in accurate and at times rapid movements. Agility is important in various tumbling movements as simply getting up and down, as well as in locomotor activities, such as jumping, hopping, skipping, and the like.

To assess agility a child may be asked to "see how fast you can get up" from a back lying position. Normally a five-year-old should take about two seconds to arise, a seven-year-old will usually get up in even less time. By the age of four a child should be able to walk and to run smoothly, coordinating arms with legs, and possessing a rhythmic and smooth tempo in his gait.

Locomotor agility can be assessed by asking a child to hop on one foot and to jump from two feet. If the child is either four or five he should be able to jump and to land with two feet reasonably well and should be able to hop two to three times on one foot. By five he should be able to jump over a rope about eight to ten inches high via a two foot take-off and land on two feet. Also by this age he should be able to execute a standing broadjump of from two to three feet, leaving and landing on both feet at the same time. By seven a child should be able to jump and to hop with greater facility and should be able to skip and to gallop. He should be able to jump from two feet and to hop into one-foot-by-one-foot squares with accuracy by the time he reaches his seventh year.

In many ways the trampoline can be used as if it were a tumbling mat. Various rolling and agility activities in which the body remains relatively close to the mat can be employed, as can agility activities involving various kinds of locomotion. Most of the standard trampoline "drops" develop agility. At the same time other tasks may be devised to enhance the agility of the body parts to integrate smoothly with each other. Examples of some of these are as follows:

1. The trampoline may be used to roll on in various ways,

28 Trampoline Activities

       i.e. the body moving along the bed while turning on its long axis.
2. From a hand and knee position, facing the long end of the trampoline, rolls may be done from side to side as shown:

3. Tumbling activities may be instituted. For example, a front roll is often easier when rolling "down hill" from near the springs on one end, particularly if the instructor's body weight depresses the bed in front of the child. Care must be taken to "spot" the back of the head as the roll is made, and to see that the child starts from a crouching position with his knees not contacting the mat.

Agility Activities 29

4. Back shoulder rolls may also be performed from near the springs at one end.
5. Arm-leg coordinations may be practiced by doing jumping jacks in the air. The additional height achieved on the trampoline, as opposed to jumping on the floor, give the child more time to coordinate the legs with the arms in this and in similar movements.

6. Variations in the jumping jack may be performed as, for example, the child attempts to move just the arm and leg on one side, and then the other side on each jump. Other times the legs may be practiced, apart and together, and the arms then practiced separately...up and down.
7. The trampoline may be utilized as part of an obstacle course, and each child may be asked to move across in different ways, either across its width or across its

30 Trampoline Activities

length. Getting on and off the trampoline is a developmental task in itself. Ways of moving across the bed bed can include "backward ways," "turning ways," "rolling ways" and the like.

Thus if the children are capable, various locomotor patterns can be practiced while traversing the bed. Hopping, jumping, walking, as well as skipping and galloping are some of the activities which may be used to traverse the surface of the trampoline.

8. Further activities may include the use of a rope. A rope may be jumped as it lies on the bed. Hi-jumping may be practiced at various heights (the safety problems inherent in this activity are obvious).

9. A rope may be held and turned by instructors standing at opposite corners of the trampoline so a child may practice rope jumping..."Mable, Mable, set the table,"... etc. It will probably be found, however, that rope jumping practice on the trampoline will not positively transfer to rope jumping on the ground, as in the latter surface an extra "get-set" jump is required between each big jump, whereas on the trampoline the depression of the bed at each descent provides the hesitation needed to time the jump to the speed of the rope.

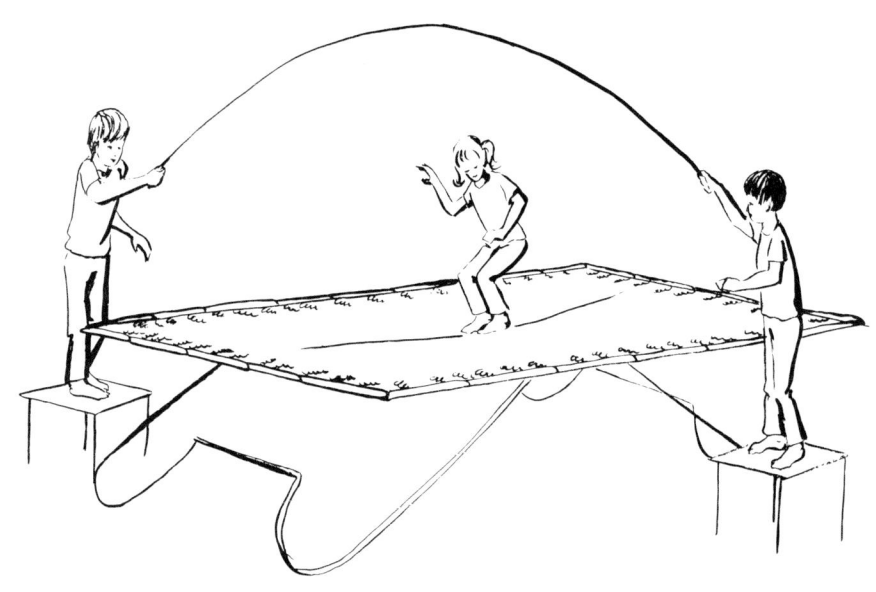

The rope turners have a responsibility, particularly during the learning process, of passing the rope under the jumper at the proper times, rather than requiring him to adjust his jumping speed and height to the speed of the rope.
10. In addition to the more difficult agility activities outlined above, simple falling to the front and to the back may be practiced on the trampoline.

SUMMARY

Agility involves the ability of the child to integrate the body parts into smooth, integrated movements involving arm, leg, body segment and locomotor integrations. The trampoline offers an excellent surface upon which to engage in various tumbling movements, locomotor activities, rope jumping, as well as arm-leg coordinations (jumping jacks).

8
The Body Image

Several clinicians have suggested that the child's body image is enhanced by trampoline bouncing. In studies we have carried out in our laboratory we found a general order in which children discover their body parts and movement capacities. Research by others has added to our knowledge of this sequence, as well as studies we have carried out with blind, retarded, neurologically impaired, and with normal children.

Some researchers have suggested that the left-right dimensions of the body, once they are acquired by the child, will somehow project themselves into space and aid in correcting letter-reversal problems. Our research has not confirmed the close association claimed by some between measures of laterality (left-right awareness) and directionality (cognizance of the left-right dimensions in space). There is indirect evidence, however, that if we teach for transfer, a child may indeed be aided in the structuring of space, after being able to properly identify left-right body parts.

Important to any sensible program of body-image training for atypical children is cognizance of the order in which normal children acquire knowledge of their body parts, and of various left-right dimensions. The sequence which follows attempts to delineate this type of developmental sequence within reasonably exact limits. The activities which follow this sequence delineate activities on the trampoline which may contribute to the acquisition of concepts within each one of the "developmental stations" contained in the sequence outlined.

	Evidenced in normal children at
Planes of the body (front, back, side, top, bottom)	2 years
Body parts (hands, legs, arms), parts of the face	
Bodily movements (jump up, bend down)	2 1/2 years

34 Trampoline Activities

Limb movements (bend arm, straighten leg)	3-4 years
Left-right body parts	5 1/2-7 years
Left-right movements	
Location of objects to the left and right	6-7 years
Locating the body, according to left-right directions ("Lie down on your left side")	
Things have a left and right, relative to the child.	7 years
Less obvious body parts, wrist, thigh, forearm, little finger, etc.	8 years
People have lefts and rights, and can make left-right movements independent of the child's personal reference system.	9-10 years

Generally normal children will continue to make errors in left-right judgements until the age of about 10 years. After that time they will make the chance errors seen in adults.

The left and right of things seems to be a concept which may be learned via a variety of movement experiences, some of which may be accomplished on the trampoline.

Planes of the body and body movements relative to these planes:

1. Various drops explained in the section which follows should aid to instill concepts of front, back, etc. Asking the child, while he is standing in one of the four squares formed by the two intersecting lines on the trampoline, to jump forward, sideward and backward should further aid in the acquisition of perceptions relative to body movements in various planes.
2. Instructions when learning the various drops, i.e. "bend the knees," when doing a knee drop, should begin to aid the child to acquire an idea of the limbs and of the limb movements possible. "Knees straight" during the seat drop, "fingers to the front" during the seat drop and similar directions should also enhance awareness of the body parts, and of their movements.
3. The concept of left and right can be accomplished in many ways using a trampoline. Jumping into the four squares can be directed by asking the child to "jump to the left,"

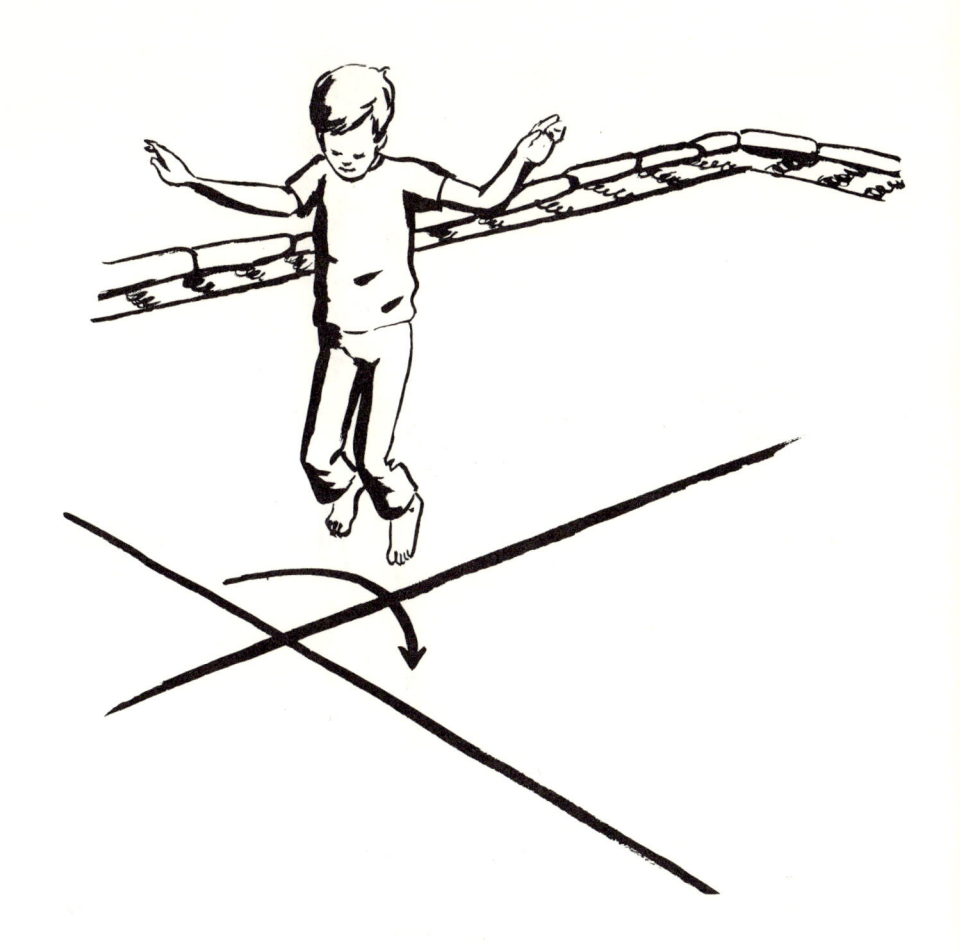

"to the left rear," "to the front right," etc. as he moves around the squares. When the child is in the middle of the trampoline he can be asked to make one-half, one-quarter and full turns to the right or to the left.

Further left-right activities can include rolling from a hand-knee position (facing the longer side of the trampoline) to the left or right.

Balance training described in a previous section can also include body image training as the child is asked to posture on his left or right foot, or to name his feet as he walks the longer line on the elastic bed.

The various agility activities described in the previous section can be employed to enhance the body image. As the child rolls, for example, he may be asked to do it slowly, so that he can call out whether he is on his left side, back, front, or right side.

Hopping the length of the trampoline, along the line, can be done on the left or right foot, or alternating feet while skipping. The child may be requested to name the foot utilized.

Jumping jack activities can be performed with one arm at a time with the child verbally identifying which arm is used.

Shoulder rolls can be carried out over the right or left shoulder, according to the instructor's directions.

SUMMARY

A child's body image may be heightened by selected activities on a trampoline. He may learn about the planes of his body as he lands on them and is asked to identify them verbally. A variety of left-right games and movements should improve his awareness of these dimensions of his physique.

Attention should be paid when engaging in these tasks to the norms presented, concerning what a child of a given age may be expected to know about his body. Aiding a child to structure space from various left-right and up-down games is possible only if transfer from the body image to space is specifically taught for, i.e. "Look Johnny, the 'd' faces toward your left hand, place your left hand on the round part of the 'd'."

9
Basic Drops

Books on trampolining invariably contain information concerning the basic drops and then lead toward the more complex tumbling activities possible. Thus in this chapter we will devote space to outlining how to perform the basic "drops" and in the sections which follow, more complex combinations of these are described. This booklet does not contain material relative to complex "air" tumbling movements, information of this nature may be found in several of the texts listed in the bibliography.

Several basic principles should be kept in mind when attempting to perform tricks on a trampoline:

1. Body segment changes should be made in the air. For example, the performer should not "kick off" the bed when bringing the feet up for a seat drop, but should assume the sitting position in the air AFTER HE HAS LEFT the bed. If a movement is anticipated and initiated when the performer is on the bed, it is likely that he will "travel" forward or backward on the bed and if the anticipatory movement is vigorous enough he could end up on the springs or on the floor!
2. Most basic tricks should start and end with the performer hitting the middle of the trampoline with his feet or some other body part. The performer's center of mass should be directly over his take-off point when leaving the bed. He should not be leaning forward or backward when leaving the bed. If he is, the pathway of his center of mass, determined by drawing an arc through his take-off point and his center of mass, may terminate on the floor!
3. When leaving the bed after each trick it is possible to gain additional lift for the next trick by vigorous upthrust of the arms and head. Sometimes this is preceded by a hand-push on the trampoline, as in a front drop, etc.
4. There are well-established, and sound progressions for the learning of both basic and advanced trampoline gymnastic stunts on the trampoline. These sequences should be rigidly adhered to in order to avoid injury.

40 Trampoline Activities

Hand-Knee Drop

The hand-knee drop is one of the simplest, and may be led up to by simply bouncing in a hand-knee position during the orientation period described previously. The child should lean forward from the feet, bend the knees after leaving the bed and lean forward, palms extended toward the mat, fingers together and shoulder-width apart. It should be attempted to contact both knees, the tops of the feet and the palms of the hands at the same time. However, it is usual, during the initial stages, that the knees hit first. However, if the child is cautioned to lean forward, it prevents a whiplash effect in the lower back which he might experience if he were to just drop to his knees with the head and shoulders slightly back of the hips.

He should regain his feet by pushing hard with the hands and leaning back slightly after leaving the bed. When contacting the bed the eyes should be up, looking slightly ahead of the hands, with the back flat. Common errors include anticipating the movement and leaning too soon and too far forward, contacting with the knees instead of the hand and knees, or jumping forward to the knees instead of permitting the knees and hands to straddle the center of the trampoline. The movement should be practiced by first having the child position himself in the middle of the trampoline in the proper hand-knee position.

Seat Drop

After first assuming a seated position in the middle of the trampoline the child should be asked to bounce, hit on his seat, backs of legs and hands, and then attempt to regain his feet. The feet, as contact is made, are higher than the hips as the body weight of the child depresses the bed under the hips more than under the feet. The feet should be together, knees straight, hands at the sides, palms contacting the mat FINGERS TOWARD THE FEET. If the hands contact the mat in the reverse position (fingers pointing backward away from the feet) it is possible that elbow hyperextension may occur as the bed of the trampoline springs back.

Care should be taken to position the feet to the front after the feet leave the bed, so that the child does not travel forward or backward. The back should be straight when contacting the bed, eyes straight ahead. Lead-up activities to the seat drop include immobile positioning in the center of the trampoline, and then having the instructor "bounce" the child to his feet; placing one foot behind him and riding the trampoline, and the pushing downward hard, lifting the child upward on the subsequent rebound. The child, as he regains his feet after this kind of help, should be assisted under the arms by the instructor.

Combinations may be made by chaining together the seat drop with the hands and knee drop previously described.

Front Drop

This drop can be dangerous and various combinations of the previous two drops should be attempted before attempting this one. For example, a "star" can be practiced, combining seat and hand-knee drops, in the following manner: Seat drop toward the short end, quarter turn left, hand-knee drop toward the long side, quarter turn left, seat drop toward the other short end, quarter turn left, to a hand-knee drop toward the other long side.

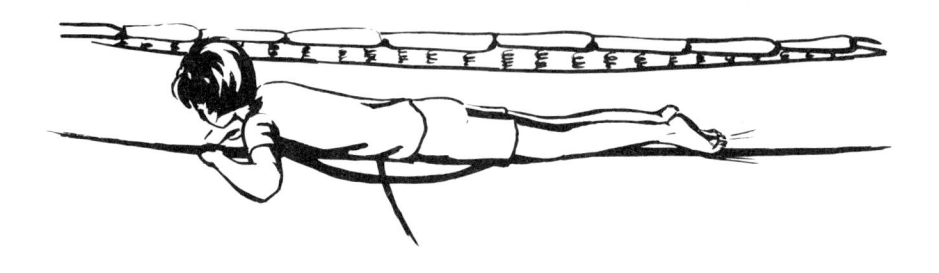

The front drop can be practiced initially from a hand-knee position with the child or the instructor pushing the bed downward in rhythm, to create a bounce. When the hands and knees clear the bed a few inches, the child should be encouraged to extend his legs to the rear and his arms to the front and to contact the bed on his stomach. The child should be cautioned not to dive forward, but should contact the center of the bed with the center of his body. The elbows should not be directly under the shoulders, but should be out to the side, with the palms of the hands directly in front of the face, facing downward so that they can push during the rebound part of the trick enabling the child to regain his feet.

Next in progression should be a drop to a hand-knee position and immediate extension to the front drop position, while the final step is to drop from a bounce to a front drop position.

Knee Drop

If the child's lower back is reasonably strong he should be encouraged to attempt a knee drop, with the upper part of the body in an upright position. The knees should bend, hand contact on the mat should be made with the tops of the feet and the front of the shins. As the body leaves the bed the arms should thrust upward to gain additional heights for the next trick. The child should be cautioned not to lean backward when contacting the mat during the drop, thus preventing hyperextension of the lower back. The lift off part of the trick should be made upward rather than forward.

Back Drop

Initially the child should be positioned in an immobile position slightly back of center on the trampoline. His feet should be at about a 45-degree angle, his hands on the front of his thighs and head slightly forward, neck muscles tight. The hands are on the front of the thighs so that when the drop is made they do not keep coming up and hit the child in the face.

The next step is to attempt a seat drop. Then, after lifting off the mat, position the legs in the 45-degree angle position, attempting to contact the flat of the back on the mat in the position described above. The usual mistake made is to not lift the legs high enough the first time, thus contacting the hips and creating a mild whiplash effect in the head and neck region. Other mistakes include not positioning the neck properly and attempting to lift the legs too soon after doing the seat drop instead of waiting for the lift from the mat. In this trick, as in the others, changes in positions of the body should be made at the top of the bounce in the air, not while going up or while coming down.

After the contact on the back is properly made, the feet are regained by vigorously pushing the thighs downward and extending the body, at the hips, at the top of the bounce. A common mistake here is to attempt the body extension too soon after the back leaves the mat, instead of again waiting until the top of the bounce is reached.

The next step is to drop back while standing on one foot, without a bounce, lifting the other foot to a 45-degree angle to initiate the drop. The final step, of course, is to execute a back-drop from a bounce, and should not be attempted until the previous two steps are over-learned.

Combinations

Combinations of these drops may be made around the body's short axis (from hip to hip), as the child remains facing in the same direction. For example, he may be asked to do a knee drop,

hand-to-knee drop, and then regain his feet. Other combinations include:
1. Seat to knee drop
2. Hand-knee drop to seat drop, to hand-knee drop
3. Hand-knee to front drop, to seat drop, to stand (a vigorous push is necessary from the front drop in order to obtain clearance permitting the feet to come under the body.)
4. Seat, back drop to the feet.
5. Hand-to-knee drop, to seat drop, to back drop to the feet.

All the stops within each of the sequences leading toward these drops should be over-learned, practiced until perfect for a number of trials, before proceeding to the next part of the sequence. This kind of over-learning is particularly necessary when working with younger children and/or retarded children whose performance is often extremely variable, and subject to momentary arousal level, attention span, and similar transitory attributes.

The basic drops described on the previous pages should be preceded by teaching children the basic positions prior to getting on the trampoline, and then on the trampoline's bed prior to "dropping" to them. These basic drops when practiced in sequence should aid serial memory ability and provide children with thinking problems involving movement.

Care should be taken to see that the child does not anticipate the various movement, as he leaves the bed, but that he "lifts" upward after each trick, and that he contacts the bed in the correct positions so as to avoid injury. These drops should be attempted only after the orientation movements described in Chapter V have been practiced.

10
Complex Combinations

Utilizing the basic drops described in the previous section, a number of combinations of tricks can be enjoyed.

A star, which was previously described, combines one-quarter turns alternating with seat and knee drops.

Combinations of the tricks in the previous section were described in which the child remained facing in the same direction, and rotated on the short axis from hip to hip. However, additional combinations are possible involving rotations on both the short and long axis.

For example, the turn table may be executed by changing from a seat drop facing toward one short end of the trampoline to a seat drop (after turning one-half turn) facing in the other direction. Intermediate steps should include a seat drop with a stiff-kneed recovery to the feet in the same direction accompanied by a vigorous arm lift with both arms, then a stiff-kneed recovery to the feet with a one-half turn to a stand in the opposite direction, and finally the completed trick, seat drop, one-half turn to a seat drop. Care should be taken to bring the body into the long axis (i.e. straighten out after the first seat drop) bringing the feet directly under the body before turning the head to gain the other seat drop. The most common error is to anticipate the second seat drop, and to make attempts which result in an improper and mechanically poor turn due to the fact that the bend is not taken out of the body prior to executing it.

A spiral may be learned by first executing a seat drop in one direction, and then turning off the bounce and executing a hand to knee drop, or front drop facing in the opposite direction. The body must be straightened by lifting the hips off the first seat drop before a turn is attempted, by turning the head, and placing the arm across the chest (left arm if turning to the right). This combination may be made more difficult by attempting to turn back (moving in the same direction) to a seat drop again, or still more difficult by executing a seat drop, arching the body, completing a whole turn around the long axis in a horizontal position, and assuming a seat drop in the same direction again.

Simple front somersaults, using the hands, may be executed from one end near the springs, and gradually transformed into a front somersault free of the bed. Initially a low somersault is executed, using the hands. After this is executed correctly, the child is urged to simply crouch, push downward with his hands and tuck the head under. This is done higher and higher (care should be taken not to do any preliminary bounces) until the head and shoulder clear the mat, and only the hands touch. After the head and shoulders clear by several inches for several trials, the child may then crouch at one end of the trampoline and jump once throwing his head under and his elbows upward and backward, initiating a rotation, which should terminate in a seat-drop position.

If the child evidences any fear or hesitation during the initial steps in this series he should not be encouraged to go to more advanced steps. More advanced tumbling stunts are described elsewhere and are beyond the scope of this text. It is unlikely, however, that many atypical children will prove capable of executing them.

Complex combinations of some of the simple tricks involve movement either on the long or short axis of the child's body. The more complicated of these may be found in the more advanced trampoline books listed in the bibliography. The ones listed here are not the more dangerous, as little somersaulting is necessary, but their correct execution requires a prolonged practice on the part of many children.

11
Thinking and Trampolining

A number of games which encourage thought can be engaged in on the trampoline. An important intellectual attribute is the ability to chain together a series of thoughts, events, words or letters. To remember is usually to remember the order of something. Seriation and perceptual span (the ability to perceive quickly a number of stimuli at the same time) are closely related.

Numerous games may involve serial-memory ability on the trampoline. For example: A simple follow-the-leader game may be played in which a child executes a series of three or four movements and a second child attempts to imitate him in the correct order. In our clinical world it has been observed that it is easiest for an observing child to instruct verbally a third child to do the same things the first child did. Next in order of difficulty is for a child to remember his own series of three or four or five movements (how many depends upon the mental age of the child. Trainable retardates seldom go beyond four, while some educables can get to five or even six). The most difficult serial memory task of this nature is for a child to imitate the four or five movements of another child which he has just observed.

Other variables influencing the facility with which a child can remember movements of this nature in a series are: the difficulty of the tasks presented, and the length of time lapsing between performance and imitation.

Task variation can also be utilized in order to tap children's intellectual capacities. After enough motor data has been inserted into a child's memory (after a number of types of possible movements have been learned) the children may be given choices of how they attempt to execute a given task within given limits. For example, reactions to such general directions as "How many things can you do after a knee drop?", or "How many backward ways can you come down the trampoline?", or "How many ways can you turn from this side of the trampoline to that side?", or perhaps "How many ways can you balance with three parts of your body touching the trampoline, one of which is your elbow?", are more

48 Trampoline Activities

likely to elicit intellectual involvement of your students, some of whom may vitally need opportunities to think, than will the usual response to the command approach often utilized.

Using the trampoline and simple apparatus such as balls, ropes and the like, children may also be encouraged to invent games. The trampoline may be utilized by itself in such situations, or may be employed with other apparatus around the gymnasium as a component of an obstacle course.

Further intellectual challenges may be offered by playing movement anagrams with some of the more gifted children. A series of letters—six or eight—may be paired with specific movements, i.e. E = jump and tuck, R = seat drop, etc. After a group of children learn the "code" they may observe each other spelling words, attempt to repeat the word spelled out in movements, and/or attempt to devise as many word-movement combinations as they can using the letters at their disposal.

Motor activities will aid a child to think to the extent to which he is encouraged to think about the motor activities in which he is engaged. The activities described in this chapter are only some of the many ways in which the trampoline may be used to encourage children's intellectual participation. Other methods will become apparent to the sensitive teacher as this type of activity is taught. Indeed the children may even teach the teacher additional learning games on the trampoline.

Appendix

CHECK LIST OF TRAMPOLINE SKILLS, AGILITY EXERCISES AND BALANCE ACTIVITIES

1. Can jump on floor with proper arm lift. _____
2. Can assume knee-drop, seat-drop, front-drop positions on mat prior to mounting trampoline. _____
3. Can assume proper knee bend when stopping jump on floor. _____
4. Can mount trampoline. _____
5. Can find center of trampoline when crawling. _____
6. Can roll down trampoline under control. _____
7. Can do hand-knee roll, over side, to hand-knee position. _____
8. Can jump in center of trampoline and stop bounce. _____
9. Can jump, execute one-half turn and stop bounce. _____
10. Can balance on one foot for two seconds, eyes open, using arms. _____
11. Can do hand-knee drop and regain feet. _____
12. Can do hand-knee to immediate front drop. _____
13. Can do seat drop and regain feet. _____
14. Can do knee drop and regain feet. _____
15. Can do knee drop. _____
16. Can do simple star, quarter turns alternating knee and seat drop. _____
17. Can do simple turns from seat to hand to knee facing in opposite direction. _____
18. Can do front roll on the trampoline. _____
19. Can jump rope on the trampoline, turned by others. _____

Trampoline Activities

20. Can do hand-knee to front drop. _____
21. Can do seat to back drop. _____
22. Can do back drop from a one foot stand, lifting other foot to proper angle. _____
23. Can do front drop from the feet to the feet. _____
24. Can do back drop from the feet to the feet. _____
25. Can execute "swivel hips" (seat drop, one half turn to seat drop). _____
26. Can engage in choice behavior on the trampoline, i.e. demonstrate original ways of turning, of traveling down bed. _____
27. Can invent original games on the trampoline. _____

Bibliography

1. Burns, Ted. Tumbling Techniques Illustrated, New York: The Ronald Press Co., 1957.
2. Cratty, Bryant J. Developmental Games for Physically Handicapped Children, Palo Alto, California: Peek Publications, 1969.
3. _____. Developmental Sequences of Perceptual-Motor Tasks, Freeport, Long Island: Educational Activities, 1967.
4. _____. Moving and Learning: 50 Vigorous Activities for the Atypical Child, Freeport, Long Island: Educational Activities, Inc., 1968.
5. _____. Motor Activity and the Education of Retardates, Philadelphia: Lea and Febiger, 1969.
6. _____. Social Dimensions of Physical Activity, Englewood Cliffs, New Jersey, 1967.
7. _____. Perceptual-Motor Behavior and Educational Processes, Springfield: Charles E. Thomas Co., 1968.
8. _____. and Sister Margaret Mary Martin. Perceptual-Motor Efficiency in Children, the Measurement and Improvement of Movement Attributes, Philadelphia: Lea and Febiger, 1969.
9. _____. Psychology and Physical Activity, Englewood Cliffs, New Jersey: Prentice-Hall, 1968.
10. Griswold, Larry. Trampoline Tumbling, St. Louis: Business Collaborators, Inc., 1958.
11. Keeney, Chuck. Trampolining Illustrated, New York: The Ronald Press Co., 1961.
12. LaDue, Frank and Jim Norman. Two Seconds of Freedom—

54 Trampoline Activities

> This is Trampolining, Cedar Rapids, Iowa: Nissen Trampoline Company, 1960.

13. Loken, N. Tumbling Instructor's Guide. Chicago: The Athletic Institute.

14. McClaw, L.L. Tumbling Illustrated. New York: A.S. Barnes & Co., 1930.